SUMMARY OF UNMASKING JEZEBEL'S INTERCESSORS

Conquer The Demonic Spirit, Hijacking What God Is Building In Your Life

JENNIFER LECLAIRE

CONTENTS

Introduction to "Summary of Unmasking Jezebel's Intercessors"	v
1. "Hello, My Name Is Jezebel"	1
2. "Intercessors of Light"	5
3. "Intercessors of Darkness"	8
4. "Why Jezebel Is Attracted to Intercession"	12
5. "Why Jezebel's Intercessors Are So Dangerous"	15
6. "Protection, Power, and Prestige"	18
7. "Prophesying, Teaching, Undermining, and Dominating"	22
8. "Grooming Sons, Spies, Messengers, and False Prophets"	25
9. "Avoiding Tapping Into Witchcraft Prayers"	28
10. "Confronting Jezebel's Intercessors"	31
11. "Dealing with Jezebel's Aftermath"	34
12. "What Jezebel's Intercessors Don't Want You to Know"	37
About the Publisher	41

INTRODUCTION TO "SUMMARY OF UNMASKING JEZEBEL'S INTERCESSORS"

Welcome to "Summary of Unmasking Jezebel's Intercessors," a concise and insightful distillation of the original work, "Unmasking Jezebel's Intercessors." This summary book serves as a guide for readers who seek to grasp the essential teachings and revelations of the full text in a more condensed format.

"Unmasking Jezebel's Intercessors" is an eye-opening exploration into the complex and often misunderstood spiritual concept of the Jezebel spirit – a topic that has intrigued and challenged believers for centuries. This book delves deeply into the biblical and spiritual aspects of Jezebel's influence, particularly focusing on its manifestation through intercessors in contemporary Christian communities.

Our aim with this summary is to provide you, the reader, with a clear and coherent understanding of the main themes, key points, and crucial insights presented in the original work. Whether you are a spiritual leader, an intercessor, or simply someone seeking deeper spiritual knowledge, this summary offers valuable lessons and strategies for recognizing and combating the subtle yet powerful influence of Jezebel's intercessors.

Through this summarized version, you will gain an understanding of the signs and characteristics of Jezebel's influence, learn the importance of discernment and spiritual warfare, and discover practical steps for safeguarding your faith community against this deceptive force.

As you journey through these pages, we hope that the distilled wisdom and guidance encapsulated here will empower you to stand firm in your faith, equipped with the knowledge and spiritual tools to face and overcome the challenges posed by Jezebel's intercessors. Let this summary be a beacon of light, guiding you to a deeper understanding and a stronger stance in your spiritual walk.

CHAPTER 1

"HELLO, MY NAME IS JEZEBEL"

Bible Verse

John 10:10 - "The thief comes only to steal and kill and destroy; I have come that they may have life, and have it to the full."

Introduction

This chapter delves into the deceptive nature of the Jezebel spirit, highlighting its tendency to infiltrate various organizations and groups, including churches and businesses, under the guise of a helpful and committed individual. The chapter emphasizes the need for discernment in identifying this spirit to prevent the harm it causes.

Word of Wisdom

"Jezebel hides behind the mask of manipulation and control, but let's be clear:

"HELLO, MY NAME IS JEZEBEL"

Jezebel is not a spirit of manipulation and control."- Jennifer LeClaire

Main Theme

The chapter focuses on understanding and identifying the Jezebel spirit, a deceptive and harmful presence that infiltrates and undermines organizations and individuals, often mistaken for assertive personalities or misidentified due to its subtle nature.

Key Points

- The Jezebel spirit infiltrates groups discreetly, often appearing helpful and committed.
- It's difficult to discern, as it hides its true destructive intentions behind a façade of helpfulness.
- Many assertive individuals are mistakenly labeled as Jezebels, leading to wrongful accusations.
- True understanding of the Jezebel spirit is crucial to avoid both deception and false accusations.
- The spirit targets the hurt and wounded, exploiting their vulnerabilities.
- Jezebel is essentially a spirit of seduction, aiming to lead people away from their faith and purpose.

Key Themes

- **Deceptive Nature of Jezebel**: The Jezebel spirit is adept at deception, presenting itself as benevolent while secretly working to undermine and destroy. It's not just manipulative but fundamentally a seducing force that misleads and corrupts.
- **The Problem of Misidentification**: Many people are wrongly accused of being influenced by the Jezebel spirit due to their assertive or strong personalities. This misidentification can cause harm to genuine individuals and hinder the true identification of the Jezebel spirit.
- **The Role of Discernment**: Proper discernment is essential to recognize the Jezebel spirit. It requires spiritual insight and wisdom to differentiate between true malevolence and mere personality traits or immature behaviors.
- **The Impact on Organizations**: The infiltration of the Jezebel spirit can have severe consequences for organizations, leading to internal strife, confusion, and a deviation from their core values and objectives.
- **Strategies for Combatting Jezebel**: Recognizing the presence of the Jezebel spirit is the first step, followed by spiritual warfare and prayer to combat its influence. Leaders must be vigilant and proactive in protecting their organizations and people from its effects.

Conclusion

Understanding the Jezebel spirit is crucial for leaders and individuals alike to protect their organizations and personal lives from its destructive influence. Proper discernment, awareness, and spiritual strategies are key to combating this deceptive and harmful force.

CHAPTER 2

"INTERCESSORS OF LIGHT"

Bible Verse

Psalm 119:105 - "Your word is a lamp for my feet, a light on my path."

Introduction

This chapter compares intercessors to lighthouse keepers, responsible for maintaining the light that guides and warns others. Emphasizing the critical role of intercessors in spiritual warfare, the author likens them to keepers of the flame, always vigilant and dedicated in their task.

Word of Wisdom

"Your faith will rise because faith comes by hearing and hearing by the Word, and your faith will cause you to outlast the enemy of your soul who is

trying to get you to give up."- Jennifer LeClaire

Main Theme

The theme revolves around the concept of intercessors as bearers of light, contrasting the darkness of Jezebel's influence with the light of Christ's intercession. It emphasizes the importance of true, persistent, and spiritually aligned intercession.

Key Points

- Intercessors serve a crucial role, akin to lighthouse keepers, guiding and warning others.
- The Word of God serves as the guiding light for intercessors.
- Differentiation between intercessors of light and darkness is vital.
- Jesus Christ is the ultimate model of an intercessor.
- Understanding and practicing true intercession is key in spiritual warfare.

Key Themes

- **Role of Intercessors**: Intercessors are likened to keepers of the flame, tasked with maintaining spiritual vigilance and guidance, much like a lighthouse keeper maintains the light to guide ships.

- **Jesus Christ as the Chief Intercessor:** Jesus' life and actions provide the ultimate model for intercessors, demonstrating the importance of prayer, sacrifice, and dedication to God's will.
- **Dichotomy of Intercession:** There's a clear contrast between the intercessors of light, who follow God's path, and the intercessors of darkness, influenced by demonic forces like Jezebel.
- **Attributes of Intercessors of Light:** These intercessors are characterized by their self-sacrifice, dedication to standing in the gap, perseverance in prayer, mercy, humility, discretion, and love-motivation.
- **The Battle Against Darkness:** Intercessors of light are engaged in a spiritual battle against the darkness brought by spirits like Jezebel, requiring them to be vigilant and rooted in God's Word.

Conclusion

Intercessors are essential in the spiritual realm, acting as beacons of light against the darkness. By emulating Christ's example and adhering to the principles of true intercession, they play a pivotal role in guiding and protecting others from spiritual harm. The chapter encourages readers to embrace this role, emphasizing the power of persistent prayer and the importance of walking in the light of Christ.

CHAPTER 3

"INTERCESSORS OF DARKNESS"

Bible Verse

1 John 1:5 - "God is light; in him there is no darkness at all."

Introduction

This chapter uses a parable about a blind man with a lamp to illustrate how intercessors of darkness, despite appearing to carry light, are actually walking in spiritual blindness and ignorance. The chapter emphasizes the importance of discerning true intercession from false, and the dangers of intercessors influenced by darkness.

Word of Wisdom

"Flesh and blood did not reveal this to me. The Holy Spirit opened my eyes to this dark reality out of the blue. It was a

sudden aha moment that I expounded upon right there in the class."- Jennifer LeClaire

Main Theme

The focus is on identifying and understanding intercessors of darkness, who, influenced by sinful actions and Jezebel's spirit, operate under false pretenses, leading to harmful consequences in spiritual communities.

Key Points

- Intercessors of darkness operate under the influence of the Jezebel spirit, often unbeknownst to themselves.
- The Holy Spirit revealed the existence of these intercessors, highlighting their contrast to true intercessors of light.
- Jezebelic intercessors often start as true intercessors but are led astray by various temptations and wounds.
- False intercessors are characterized by traits like deceit, treachery, and an intention to mislead.
- Inner vows made in moments of pain or anger can lead intercessors towards darkness.
- It's vital for intercessors to be aware of their own vulnerabilities to darkness and seek God's light.

Key Themes

- **Transformation into Darkness**: True intercessors can become dark intercessors through hurts, wounds, or temptations. Jezebel targets these vulnerable individuals, transforming their intercession into a tool for her agenda.
- **Inner Vows and Jezebel's Influence**: Inner vows, often made in response to hurt or anger, can invite demonic influences like Jezebel, turning well-meaning intercessors towards dark purposes.
- **Difficulty in Discerning Darkness**: Recognizing darkness within oneself or others is challenging, necessitating a reliance on the Holy Spirit for discernment and guidance.
- **The Deception of False Intercession**: Intercessors of darkness are often unaware of their own state, believing they are serving God while actually being influenced by demonic spirits.
- **The Importance of Self-Examination and Repentance**: Intercessors must continually examine their hearts and motives, seeking God's light to ensure they are not unknowingly walking in darkness.

Conclusion

Intercessors play a crucial role in spiritual communities, but they must be vigilant against influences of darkness, particularly those of the Jezebel spirit. Recognizing and understanding the traits of dark intercessors is essential, as is self-examination and reliance on the Holy Spirit for guidance and repentance. The chapter serves as a call to guard against the subtleties of spiritual darkness and to constantly seek God's light and truth.

CHAPTER 4

"WHY JEZEBEL IS ATTRACTED TO INTERCESSION"

Bible Verse

Luke 18:9-14 - This passage illustrates the contrast between self-righteousness and humility in prayer, embodying the distinction between true intercession and the deceptive practices of Jezebelic intercessors.

Introduction

The chapter begins with a narrative about Holly, an intercessor whose pious exterior masked a Jezebelic influence, highlighting the subtlety and danger of such characters in prayer communities.

Word of Wisdom

"Jezebel knows one of the best ways to hijack prayer is to hijack intercessors."- Jennifer LeClaire

Main Theme

The main focus is on the reasons Jezebel spirits are drawn to intercessory prayer environments, exploiting vulnerabilities and seeking control, influence, and admiration through deceptive means.

Key Points

- Jezebelic intercessors initially appear pious and committed, making them difficult to discern.
- They often seek and gain positions of influence within prayer communities.
- These intercessors manipulate and control prayer meetings and participants.
- They use prayer as a platform for self-promotion and to spread gossip.
- Jezebelic intercessors exploit personal information and prayer requests for their own gain.
- Their ultimate goal is to gain admiration and control over others.

Key Themes

- **Manipulation Under Guise of Piety**: Jezebelic intercessors present themselves as devout, yet their true intent is manipulation and control, often disguised under a veneer of holiness.

- **Seeking Positions of Influence**: They gravitate towards leadership roles within prayer groups to exert control and influence the direction and focus of prayers.
- **Exploitation of Personal Information**: Jezebelic intercessors use prayer meetings to gather personal information, which they then exploit to manipulate and control individuals and situations.
- **Desire for Admiration and Authority**: A hallmark of these intercessors is their desire for admiration and recognition, often seeking to be the focal point in prayer groups and communities.
- **Combating Jezebelic Influence**: The chapter emphasizes the importance of discernment and guarding against the Jezebel spirit in prayer groups, encouraging leaders to be vigilant and proactive.

Conclusion

The chapter serves as a warning and guide to identifying and combating the Jezebel spirit within intercessory prayer circles. It underscores the importance of discernment, genuine motives in prayer, and the need for leaders to be aware of and address the influence of such deceptive individuals in their communities.

CHAPTER 5

"WHY JEZEBEL'S INTERCESSORS ARE SO DANGEROUS"

Bible Verse

Revelation 2:22-23 (CEV) - This passage highlights the severity of Jesus' warnings against those who follow Jezebel, emphasizing the peril of being influenced by her false teachings and actions.

Introduction

The chapter begins with the author's discussion with Dr. Sharon Stone about starting prophetic training in London, which leads to an encounter with a Jezebelic intercessor, underscoring the hidden dangers they pose.

Word of Wisdom

"Jezebel's intercessors are not moving in the spirit of prayer. Jezebel's intercessors are moving in a wicked spirit that's been plaguing the earth for thousands of years."- Jennifer LeClaire

Main Theme

The primary focus is on the perils posed by Jezebel's intercessors in spiritual communities, detailing their deceptive tactics, false prophecies, and harmful influences.

Key Points

- Jezebelic intercessors often disguise their true motives, making them difficult to discern.
- They use false prophecies to manipulate and divide communities.
- These intercessors can release witchcraft prayers, aiming to control people and situations.
- They have a political spirit, seeking power and control over others.
- Jezebelic intercessors can discredit true intercessors, damaging their reputations.
- They are spiritually castrated by Jezebel, losing their resistance to her influence.

Key Themes

- **False Prophecy and Manipulation**: Jezebelic intercessors often use false prophecies to manipulate others, leading them astray from God's will and creating division within communities.
- **Political Spirit and Power Dynamics**: These intercessors are driven by a political

spirit, seeking to dominate and control others, often causing confusion and discord in their pursuit of power.
- **Witchcraft Prayers and Control**: Their prayers are often guided by their own will rather than God's, attempting to control situations and people, which is a form of spiritual witchcraft.
- **Discrediting and Reputation Damage**: Jezebel's intercessors work to discredit and disgrace true intercessors, attacking their character and standing in the community.
- **Spiritual Castration and Loss of Resistance**: They are often spiritually weakened by Jezebel's influence, losing their ability to resist her manipulative tactics and becoming her tools.

Conclusion

Jezebel's intercessors pose a significant threat to spiritual communities due to their hidden agendas, manipulative tactics, and harmful influences. Recognizing and combating these dangerous elements requires discernment, vigilance, and a commitment to God's truth and righteousness.

CHAPTER 6

"PROTECTION, POWER, AND PRESTIGE"

Bible Verse

Matthew 7:15-20 (NKJV) - This passage emphasizes the importance of discerning false prophets by their fruits, which is pertinent in identifying the deceptive nature of Jezebel's intercessors.

Introduction

The chapter starts with an account of Janice, an intense intercessor whose fervent prayers hide deep emotional instability and sinful actions, revealing a Jezebelic influence at play.

Word of Wisdom

"Witchcraft prayers, which we'll discuss in another chapter, can sound accu-

rate but can defy the will of God."-
Jennifer LeClaire

Main Theme

The chapter delves into the characteristics of Jezebel's intercessors, focusing on their quest for protection, power, and prestige within spiritual communities, and the destructive consequences of their actions.

Key Points

- • Jezebel's intercessors often seek close proximity to leaders for protection and influence.
- • They exhibit traits of political and power-hungry spirits, aiming for control.
- • These intercessors may engage in witchcraft prayers, prioritizing their will over God's.
- • They attempt to create divisions within groups for personal gain or manipulation.
- • Jezebel's intercessors resist correction, often reacting defensively or with false repentance.

Key Themes

- **Subtle Motivations for Proximity**: Jezebel's intercessors strive to be close to leaders, not out of genuine respect or support, but to gain protection and influence for their hidden agendas.
- **Divide and Conquer Strategy**: They intentionally create divisions and strife within groups, utilizing manipulative tactics to disrupt unity and hinder collective spiritual growth.
- **Resistance to Correction and False Repentance**: These intercessors often exhibit an inability to accept correction, responding with defensiveness or insincere apologies while continuing their destructive behaviors.
- **Seeking Attention and Recognition**: Driven by a desire for acknowledgment, Jezebel's intercessors engage in attention-seeking behaviors, often taking credit for communal prayer achievements.
- **Power and Prestige as Driving Forces**: The pursuit of power and a commanding position within spiritual communities is a hallmark of Jezebel's intercessors, leading to disruptive and divisive actions.

Conclusion

The chapter warns of the dangers posed by Jezebel's intercessors in spiritual communities. Their hidden motives for protection, power, and prestige can lead to division, manipulation, and spiritual disruption. Discernment and vigilance are crucial in identifying and addressing these harmful influences.

CHAPTER 7

"PROPHESYING, TEACHING, UNDERMINING, AND DOMINATING"

Bible Verse

Revelation 2:20 (TPT) - This verse highlights the deceitful and destructive nature of Jezebel's intercessors, who seduce and mislead through false teachings and prophecies.

Introduction

The chapter recounts a disruptive event during an open mic night at a prayer meeting, setting the stage for a discussion on the characteristics of Jezebel's intercessors and their impact on spiritual communities.

Word of Wisdom

"If the Body of Christ would spend more time pursuing Jesus the Prophet instead of every other self-proclaimed prophet, we would be less

likely to fall into Jezebel's snare."- Jennifer LeClaire

Main Theme

This chapter explores the tactics of Jezebel's intercessors, focusing on their propensity to prophesy, teach, undermine, and dominate within spiritual settings, and the importance of discerning and addressing these behaviors.

Key Points

• Jezebel's intercessors often use prophecy and teaching to manipulate and gain influence.

• They seek to dominate and control intercessory prayer sessions.

• These intercessors are prone to criticizing others and undermining leadership authority.

• They are characterized by being offensive, easily offended, and competitive.

• Their actions can cause significant disruption and division within spiritual communities.

Key Themes

- **Jezebel's Manipulative Use of Prophecy and Teaching**: Jezebel's intercessors use prophecy and teaching not as means of genuine spiritual guidance, but as tools to manipulate and control others, often leading them away from God's truth.

- **Dominating Behavior in Prayer Settings**: These intercessors strive to control and dominate prayer sessions, often disregarding established protocols and the guidance of the Holy Spirit.
- **Critical Nature and Undermining of Authority**: Jezebel's intercessors frequently exhibit a critical nature, challenging and undermining the authority of spiritual leaders and creating division within the community.
- **Tendency to be Offensive and Competitive**: Their actions are marked by a desire to be the center of attention, leading to competitive and offensive behaviors that disrupt the harmony and focus of prayer groups.
- **Risk of Division and Disruption**: The presence of Jezebel's intercessors in spiritual settings poses a significant risk of causing division and disruption, emphasizing the need for discernment and firm leadership.

Conclusion

The chapter emphasizes the importance of recognizing and addressing the harmful influence of Jezebel's intercessors in spiritual communities. Their manipulative and dominating behaviors, if unchecked, can lead to significant disruption and division, underscoring the need for vigilant discernment and strong leadership in prayer groups.

CHAPTER 8

"GROOMING SONS, SPIES, MESSENGERS, AND FALSE PROPHETS"

Bible Verse

Revelation 2:20-23 (NLT) - This verse underlines the deceptive and manipulative nature of Jezebel and her followers, highlighting the destructive impact they have on those around them.

Introduction

The chapter opens with a cautionary tale about a potential hire for a worship director position, which reveals the manipulative influence of his wife with a Jezebel spirit. The story serves as a springboard to discuss various tactics employed by Jezebel's intercessors.

Word of Wisdom

"Not everything that glitters is gold. Sometimes, Jezebel is hiding behind the glitter."- Jennifer LeClaire

Main Theme

The chapter focuses on the various roles and strategies of Jezebel's intercessors, such as grooming spiritual sons and daughters, deploying spies and messengers, and acting as false prophets. It emphasizes the importance of discernment in identifying and dealing with these manipulative individuals.

Key Points

• Jezebel's intercessors groom spiritual sons and daughters to spread their influence and teachings.

• They deploy spies to gather information and wield it as power.

• These intercessors use unsuspecting individuals as messengers to advance their agendas.

• They exhibit strong intimidation tactics and engage in spiritual abuse.

• Their seductive nature often leads them to falsely claim prophetic gifts.

• They desire platforms to perform and gain recognition, often at the expense of others.

Key Themes

- **Jezebel's Recruitment of Followers**:
  Jezebel's intercessors actively recruit
  spiritual sons and daughters to propagate
  their deceptive teachings and expand their

influence, creating a network of loyal followers.

- **The Role of Spies in Jezebel's Network**: These intercessors often act as spies, gathering personal and sensitive information to manipulate and control situations to their advantage.
- **Use of Messengers for Manipulation**: Jezebel's intercessors strategically use messengers to communicate their intentions and spread their influence, often without the messengers realizing their role in the scheme.
- **Intimidation and Spiritual Abuse**: These individuals employ intimidation and spiritual abuse to control and manipulate others, often leaving lasting psychological and spiritual damage.
- **Seduction and False Prophecy**: They frequently claim prophetic abilities to lend credibility to their manipulations, seducing followers with false promises and guidance.

Conclusion

The chapter concludes by stressing the importance of vigilance and discernment in spiritual communities to identify and address the harmful influence of Jezebel's intercessors. Their tactics of grooming, spying, messaging, and false prophecy can cause significant disruption and harm, making it crucial to recognize and confront these behaviors guided by spiritual wisdom and insight.

CHAPTER 9

"AVOIDING TAPPING INTO WITCHCRAFT PRAYERS"

Bible Verse

Ephesians 6:12 - This verse reminds us of the spiritual nature of our battles and the importance of discerning the spiritual forces at work in our prayers and intercessions.

Introduction

The chapter opens with a troubling incident during a prayer session for Ukraine, where a Jezebel-influenced intercessor disrupted the prayer with curses against Russia. This sets the stage for a discussion on the nature of witchcraft prayers and how Christians can unwittingly engage in them.

Word of Wisdom

"Not everything that glitters is gold. Sometimes, Jezebel is hiding behind the glitter."- Jennifer LeClaire

Main Theme

The chapter focuses on the dangers of witchcraft prayers, emphasizing that prayers motivated by self-will rather than God's will can inadvertently release negative spiritual forces. It underscores the need for discernment in prayer and the importance of aligning our prayers with God's will.

Key Points

- Witchcraft prayers can be unintentionally made by Christians when they pray against God's will.

- These prayers are often driven by the flesh rather than the Spirit.

- They can take the form of curses, selfish ambitions, or control attempts.

- Such prayers can cause harm and open doors for enemy attacks.

- Recognizing and avoiding witchcraft prayers requires discernment and spiritual maturity.

- True Christian prayer should seek God's will and be rooted in love and faith.

Key Themes

- **Nature of Witchcraft Prayers**:
  Witchcraft prayers in a Christian context are those that are self-willed, seeking to impose one's desires rather than seeking God's will. They can manifest as benign or malignant in their impact.

- **Jezebel's Influence on Prayer**: Jezebel's intercessors often engage in prayers that attempt to manipulate or control situations and people, contrary to God's will and plan.
- **The Dangers of Carnal Prayers**: Prayers that emanate from the flesh, rather than the Spirit, can inadvertently align with demonic purposes, creating openings for spiritual attacks.
- **Recognizing and Overcoming Witchcraft Prayers**: Identifying and avoiding witchcraft prayers involves a deep understanding of God's will, humility, and a heart aligned with God's purposes.
- **Repentance and Reformation**: The chapter emphasizes the need for repentance from any engagement in witchcraft prayers and reformation of prayer life to align with God's will and character.

Conclusion

The chapter concludes by emphasizing the importance of discernment and alignment with God's will in prayer. It highlights the responsibility of Christians to ensure that their prayers are motivated by faith, love, and submission to God, avoiding any form of spiritual manipulation or control that resembles witchcraft. This alignment is essential for effective, God-honoring intercession.

CHAPTER 10

"CONFRONTING JEZEBEL'S INTERCESSORS"

Bible Verse

Luke 8:17 - This verse emphasizes the revelation of hidden things and the uncovering of truth, which aligns with the theme of confronting the deceptive tactics of Jezebel's intercessors.

Introduction

The chapter narrates a challenging situation in a church where a woman, Earlene, was covertly undermining the church's ministry. Despite efforts to counsel and help her, she continued her destructive behaviors, leading to a critical confrontation.

Word of Wisdom

"When you tolerate that spirit, Jesus has issues with you. It opens a portal of hell over your life."- Jennifer LeClaire

"CONFRONTING JEZEBEL'S INTERCESSORS"

Main Theme

The focus is on the necessity of confronting individuals influenced by the Jezebel spirit within church communities. It stresses the importance of discerning and addressing such issues for the health and spiritual well-being of the congregation.

Key Points

• Jezebel's intercessors can cause severe disruption and division within a church.

• Such individuals often operate covertly, making confrontation challenging.

• Leaders must be discerning and courageous in addressing these issues.

• Direct confrontation is sometimes necessary to protect the church's integrity.

• The ultimate goal is restoration, but it requires repentance from the influenced individual.

• Failing to confront Jezebel's spirit can lead to greater spiritual harm and division.

Key Themes

- **The Subtlety of Jezebel's Influence**: Jezebel's intercessors often operate in hidden ways, making them hard to detect. They may appear helpful and committed, but they are manipulative and destructive.
- **The Impact on the Church Community**: The presence of a Jezebel spirit can cause division, spread false

teachings, and create an unhealthy church environment. It often targets vulnerable individuals.
- **The Role of Church Leadership in Confrontation**: Church leaders play a crucial role in identifying and confronting Jezebel's intercessors. This requires wisdom, spiritual discernment, and courage.
- **The Process of Confrontation and Restoration**: Confrontation should be aimed at restoration, but it demands honesty and directness. It's important to differentiate between the person and the influencing spirit.
- **The Consequences of Inaction**: Failing to address the issue can lead to further harm to the church's spiritual health and can hinder its mission and growth.

Conclusion

Confronting Jezebel's intercessors is a complex and sensitive task that requires a balance of firmness and compassion. It's imperative for the health of the church community and must be approached with prayer, wisdom, and guided by the Holy Spirit. While the ultimate goal is restoration, it must come with a genuine change in behavior and attitude from the influenced individual. Ignoring or tolerating such behavior can have detrimental effects on the church's spiritual well-being.

CHAPTER 11

"DEALING WITH JEZEBEL'S AFTERMATH"

Bible Verse

Luke 8:17 - This verse emphasizes the importance of revealing hidden truths, which is crucial in dealing with the aftermath of Jezebel's influence.

Introduction

The chapter begins with a vivid analogy of the destruction caused by atomic bombs in Japan to describe the profound impact of Jezebel's influence in a church. It highlights the necessity of addressing the aftermath of such spiritual warfare.

Word of Wisdom

"You can't always trust people, but you can certainly always trust Him [God]. Don't close your heart to people. That's

just what Jezebel wants."- Jennifer LeClaire

Main Theme

The focus of the chapter is on the critical steps and strategies necessary for healing and rebuilding after the disruptive influence of Jezebel's intercessors in a church or community.

Key Points

• The aftermath of Jezebel's influence can have long-lasting and far-reaching effects.

• Immediate responses might not reveal the full extent of the damage.

• Victims of Jezebel's influence may face ostracism and hardship.

• Leaders must remain vigilant and discerning even after addressing the primary issue.

• The healing process involves both spiritual and communal efforts.

Key Themes

- **The Ripple Effect of Jezebel's Influence**: The influence of Jezebel can continue to manifest long after the primary issue is addressed, often in subtle and

unexpected ways, requiring continued vigilance and discernment.
- **Healing and Rebuilding the Community**: Post-confrontation, it is essential to focus on healing the wounds inflicted by Jezebel's intercessors, which involves counseling, inner healing, and a strong community support system.
- **The Importance of Vigilance and Wisdom**: Leaders need to stay alert and wise to prevent further infiltration and to identify any remaining negative influences or vulnerabilities within the community.
- **Forgiveness and Moving Forward**: Part of the healing process involves forgiveness, both for those directly affected and the wider community, to prevent bitterness and facilitate a healthy environment for growth.
- **The Role of Prayer and Spiritual Authority**: Prayer and exercising spiritual authority are crucial in overcoming the aftermath of Jezebel's influence, helping to cleanse the atmosphere and bring divine guidance and restoration.

Conclusion

Dealing with Jezebel's aftermath is a complex process that requires patience, vigilance, spiritual discernment, and a heart for restoration. Leaders must be proactive in healing and rebuilding their communities, ensuring that the negative influences are thoroughly addressed. Forgiveness and prayer play pivotal roles in overcoming the challenges and moving forward with strength and unity.

CHAPTER 12

"WHAT JEZEBEL'S INTERCESSORS DON'T WANT YOU TO KNOW"

Bible Verse

2 Corinthians 2:11 - "Lest Satan should take advantage of us; for we are not ignorant of his devices." This verse emphasizes the importance of being aware of the enemy's strategies, aligning with the chapter's theme of understanding the nature of Jezebel's intercessors.

Introduction

This chapter reflects on the author's experiences and learnings about the spirit of Jezebel, emphasizing the necessity of understanding its true nature and tactics to effectively combat it in spiritual warfare.

Word of Wisdom

"An enemy exposed is an enemy defeated." This quote underscores the power of awareness and knowledge in overcoming

spiritual adversaries like Jezebel's intercessors.- Jennifer LeClaire

Main Theme

The chapter focuses on demystifying the spirit of Jezebel, offering insights into its true nature, strategies, and how it manifests in both individuals and churches.

Key Points

• Jezebel is more than just a spirit of control and manipulation; it's primarily a spirit of seduction.

• The name Jezebel signifies un-exalted and unwilling to cohabitate or share power.

• There are two Jezebels in Scripture to show the spirit's long-standing influence.

• Jezebel targets prophets and intercessors because they are key conduits of God's voice and power.

• Christians can be influenced by Jezebel but not possessed by it, as it's a principality.

• Jezebel's master plan is to seduce believers away from true faith and lead them into sin and heresy.

Key Themes

- **Understanding the True Nature of Jezebel**: Jezebel is a seductive force that leads people away from truth and into error, going beyond mere control and manipulation.
- **Historical and Biblical Context of Jezebel**: Jezebel's origins in Scripture and her association with antinomianism and idolatry show her long-term impact on faith and morality.
- **The Danger of Misidentifying Jezebel**: Mislabeling behaviors or individuals as 'Jezebel' without proper understanding can lead to harmful consequences and overlook the true issues at hand.
- **Strategies to Counteract Jezebel's Influence**: Spiritual discernment, prayer, and understanding Jezebel's tactics are crucial in preventing and combating her influence in churches and individual lives.
- **The Process of Deliverance from Jezebel's Influence**: Healing from the wounds that give Jezebel a stronghold is key, alongside scriptural knowledge and spiritual support.

Conclusion

Recognizing and understanding the spirit of Jezebel is crucial for effective spiritual warfare. This knowledge equips believers to identify, confront, and overcome Jezebel's deceptive tactics. The chapter emphasizes the importance of awareness,

"WHAT JEZEBEL'S INTERCESSORS DON'T WANT ...

scriptural understanding, and spiritual discernment in dealing with Jezebel's influence.

FAITH AND FLAME PRESS
IGNITING THE FLAMES OF FAITH

Faith and Flame Press is a Christian book publishing company that is passionate about igniting the flames of faith in the hearts of readers around the world. Our mission is to publish books that inspire, enlighten, and uplift the spirit, and help readers deepen their understanding of their faith and spirituality.

At Faith and Flame Press, we believe that books have the power to transform lives and to shape the world we live in. That's why we are committed to publishing books that are not only spiritually uplifting but also intellectually stimulating, well-researched, and thought-provoking.

www.ingramcontent.com/pod-product-compliance
Lightning Source LLC
LaVergne TN
LVHW051529070426
835507LV00023B/3378